John Kember and Sam Lewis

# Trumpet Sight-Reading

## Déchiffrage pour le trompette
## Vom-Blatt-Spiel auf der trompete

*A fresh approach / Nouvelle approche*
*Eine erfrischend neue Methode*

ED 13478
ISMN M-2201-3351-0
ISBN 978-1-84761-274-8

www.schott-music.com

Mainz · London · Madrid · New York · Paris · Prague · Tokyo · Toronto

ED 13478

British Library Cataloguing-in-Publication Data.
A catalogue record for this book is available from the British Library
ISMN M-2201-3351-0
ISBN 978-1-84761-274-8

French translation: Michaëla Rubi
German translation: Heike Brühl
Music setting and page layout by Bev Wilson
Cover Design by www.adamhaystudio.com
Printed in Germany S&Co.8814

# Contents
## Sommaire/Inhalt

# Preface

Trumpet Sight-Reading aims to establish good practice and provide a comprehensive source of material to enable the player to prepare for this most important skill. Ideally, sight-reading in some form should become a regular part of a student's routine each time they play.

This book offers the opportunity to establish the habit from the earliest stages of playing and follows a logical sequence of progression in range of notes, variety of times, keys and rhythms to cover the whole spectrum of trumpet playing including transposition.

A glossary of musical terms is provided to help the student to learn them and those used are given at the introduction to each section.

There are 11 sections beginning with the option to begin on either C or G and with basic note values. Phrasing, dynamics, rhythms and articulations are introduced gradually as are terms of tempo and expression. The emphasis is on providing idiomatic tunes and structures rather than sterile sight-reading exercises. Each section begins with several solo examples and concludes with duets and accompanied pieces, enabling the player to gain experience of sight-reading within the context of ensemble playing.

The value of duets in this book cannot be overemphasised as it gives the opportunity to listen to another player, aids good time keeping and assists with intonation and the development of a good tone. The final pieces at the end of each section offer the chance to read a short piece with a piano accompaniment.

**Section 1** uses notes C, E and G with the option of starting on either the C or the G, together with simple rhythms and time signatures.

**Section 2** introduces notes C – G with mainly stepwise movement and repeated notes. 4/4 and 2/4 time signatures.

**Section 3** retains the same 5 notes with the addition of F♯ and the key signature of G major. 3/4 time is introduced along with the dotted minim and dotted crotchet.

**Section 4** extends the range to one octave C – C together with B♭, F major, quavers and more dotted rhythms.

**Section 5** extends the range further to E♭ and F with new keys D, E♭, A and B♭ majors. 3/8 and 6/8 time signatures are introduced as are slurred quavers.

**Section 6** begins with pieces in compound time, introduces more minor keys and D♭ major. Semiquavers in simple time, more slurs and some triplets are used, and the range extended. Both dynamics and performance directions are introduced.

**Section 7** concentrates on swing style, with swing quavers throughout and a few triplet figures.

**Section 8** brings together a variety of styles, keys and rhythms previously introduced.

**Section 9** introduces simple transpositions both up and down a tone. Some chromatic and modal examples follow, together with pieces in 5/4 and 5/8.

**Section 10** begins with further exercises in transposition, a number of dance styles, the whole tone scale and the time signatures of 7/4 and 7/8.

**Section 11** makes use of all keys, double sharps and flats, a range of styles from baroque to atonal and a fully extended range.

## To the pupil: why sight-reading?

Apart from the fact that some examination boards require a test of reading at sight, whenever you are faced with a new piece, whether at home or in a lesson or audition, there is no one there to help you – only yourself! The ability to read the time and notes correctly and to observe the phrasing and dynamics quickly is probably the most important skill for you to acquire.

The aim of the book is to help you to teach yourself. The book gives guidance on what to look for and how best to prepare in a very short time by observing the time and key signatures, the shape of the melody and the marks of expression. These short pieces progress gradually to help you build up your confidence and observation and enable you to sight-read accurately. At the end of each section there are duets to play with your teacher or friends and pieces with piano accompaniment, which will test your ability to sight-read while something else is going on. This is a necessary skill when playing with a band, orchestra or other ensemble.

If you sight-read something every time you play your trumpet you will be amazed how much better you will become. Remember, if you can sight-read most of the tunes you are asked to learn you will be able to concentrate on the 'tricky bits' and complete them quickly.

Think of the tunes in this book as 'mini-pieces' and try to learn them quickly and correctly. Then when you are faced with real sight-reading you will be well equipped to succeed on a first attempt.

*You are on your own now!*

# Préface

« Déchiffrage pour la trompette » a été conçu afin de constituer un bon entraînement et proposer une source complète de matériaux permettant à l'instrumentiste de se préparer à cette compétence particulièrement importante. Idéalement, quelle qu'en soit la forme, le déchiffrage devrait faire partie intégrante des exercices pratiqués par les élèves à chaque fois qu'ils prennent leur instrument.

Cet ouvrage offre l'occasion d'instaurer l'habitude du déchiffrage dès les premiers stades de la pratique instrumentale. Il suit une séquence logique de progression en termes de notes, tempos, tonalités et rythmes et aborde tous les aspects de la pratique de la trompette, y compris la transposition.

Un glossaire des termes musicaux permettra aux élèves de les apprendre. Les termes utilisés sont indiqués au début de chaque section correspondante.

Les sections sont au nombre de onze, chacune permettant de commencer sur *do* ou *sol* et avec des valeurs de notes basiques. Le phrasé, les nuances, le rythme et les articulations sont introduits graduellement ainsi que les indications de tempo et d'expression. L'accent a été mis sur des airs et des structures idiomatiques plutôt que sur des exercices stériles de déchiffrage. Chaque partie commence par différents exemples pour trompette seule et se termine par des duos et une pièce accompagnée, permettant ainsi à l'instrumentiste d'acquérir l'expérience du déchiffrage dans le contexte de la musique d'ensemble.

On ne soulignera jamais assez l'importance des duos figurant dans ce recueil, car ils sont l'occasion d'écouter un autre instrumentiste et favorisent la régularité du tempo ainsi que la justesse de l'intonation et le développement d'un joli son. Les pièces situées à la fin de chaque section permettent de lire une pièce courte avec accompagnement de piano.

**La section 1** utilise les notes *do*, *ré* et *sol* avec la possibilité de commencer soit sur le *do* soit sur le *sol*, sur des rythmes et des mesures simples.

**La section 2** introduit toutes les notes de *do* à *sol*, la plupart du temps en mouvement conjoint et en notes répétées. Les mesures sont à 4/4 et 2/4.

**La section 3** reprend les cinq notes précédentes en y ajoutant le *fa*♯ et la tonalité de *sol* majeur et introduit la mesure à 3/4 ainsi que la blanche et la noire pointées.

**La section 4** élargit l'étendue jusqu'à l'octave, de *do* à *do*, et introduit le *si*♭, les croches et d'autres rythmes pointés.

**La section 5** poursuit la progression en ajoutant le *mi*♭ et le *fa* ainsi que les nouvelles tonalités de *ré*, *mi*♭, *la* et *si*♭ majeur, avec introduction des mesures à 3/8 et 6/8 et des croches liées.

**La section 6** commence par des pièces en ternaire. Elle introduit davantage de tonalités mineures ainsi que celle de *ré*♭ majeur. Elle fait appel aux doubles croches en mesure binaire, à davantage de liaisons et aux triolets. L'étendue est encore

augmentée et des indications à la fois de jeu et de nuances sont introduites.

**La section 7** se concentre sur un style swingué avec des croches toujours swinguées et quelques triolets.

**La section 8** rassemble une palette de styles, de tonalités et de rythmes introduits précédemment.

**La section 9** aborde des transpositions simples, un ton au dessus et un ton en dessous. Suivent quelques exemples de chromatismes et de modalité, ainsi que des pièces à 5/4 et à 5/8.

**La section 10** propose d'autres exercices de transposition et différents styles de danses, sur toute l'étendue des notes et dans des mesures à 7/4 et 7/8.

**La section 11** utilise toutes les tonalités, le double dièse et double bémol, une série de styles allant du baroque à la musique atonale, sur toute l'étendue des notes.

## A l'élève : Pourquoi le déchiffrage ?

Outre les épreuves de déchiffrages exigées par certains jurys, lorsque vous vous retrouvez face à une pièce nouvelle, que ce soit chez vous, en cours ou lors d'une audition, il n'y a personne pour vous aider – à part vous ! La capacité de lire correctement les notes et la mesure, et d'observer rapidement le phrasé et les nuances est probablement la compétence la plus importante que vous puissiez acquérir.

Ce recueil se propose de vous aider à vous entraîner vous-même. Il vous oriente sur ce que vous devez repérer et sur la meilleure manière de vous préparer en un laps de temps très court en sachant observer les indications de mesure et l'armure à la clef de la tonalité, les contours de la mélodie et les indications expressives. Ces pièces brèves, en progressant par étapes, vous feront prendre de l'assurance, aiguiseront vos observations et vous permettront de lire à vue avec exactitude et aisance. A la fin de chaque section figurent des duos que vous pourrez jouer avec votre professeur ou des amis et des morceaux avec accompagnement de piano qui mettront à l'épreuve votre habileté à déchiffrer pendant que se déroule une autre partie. Celle-ci est indispensable pour jouer dans un groupe, un orchestre ou un ensemble.

Vous serez surpris de vos progrès si vous déchiffrez une pièce à chaque fois que vous vous mettez au trompette. N'oubliez pas que si vous êtes capable de lire à vue la plupart des morceaux que vous allez étudier, vous pourrez vous concentrer sur les passages difficiles et les assimiler plus vite.

Considérez ces pages comme des « mini-morceaux » et essayez de les apprendre rapidement et sans erreur de manière à ce que, devant un véritable déchiffrage, vous soyez bien armé pour réussir dès la première lecture.

*A vous seul de jouer maintenant !*

# Vorwort

Die Stücke in Trumpet Sight-Reading sind nicht nur gute Übungen, sondern stellen auch eine umfassende Einführung in die wichtige Fähigkeit des Vom-Blatt-Lesens dar. Das Vom-Blatt-Spiel sollte zu einem festen Bestandteil im Übungsprogramm des Schülers werden, wann immer er sein Instrument in die Hand nimmt.

Das Buch bietet die Möglichkeit, sich das Vom-Blatt-Spiel von Anfang an anzugewöhnen. Neue Noten, Taktarten, Tonarten und Rhythmen werden in einer logischen Reihenfolge eingeführt, um das gesamte Spektrum des Trompetenspiels einschließlich Transposition abzudecken.

Ein Glossar mit musikalischen Begriffen soll den Schülern beim Erlernen dieser Begriffe helfen. Die verwendeten Begriffe werden zu Beginn jedes Teils genannt.

Das Buch besteht aus elf Teilen. Man beginnt entweder mit C oder G und einfachen Notenwerten. Nach und nach werden Phrasierung, Dynamik, Rhythmen und Artikulation sowie Tempo- und Vortragsangaben eingeführt. Der Schwerpunkt liegt auf authentischen Melodien und Strukturen statt auf sterilen Vom-Blatt-Leseübungen. Jeder Teil beginnt mit mehreren Solobeispielen und endet mit Duetten und begleiteten Stücken, die dem Schüler die Möglichkeit bieten, beim gemeinsamen Musizieren Erfahrungen im Vom-Blatt-Spiel zu sammeln.

Die Duette in diesem Buch haben einen hohen Stellenwert, da sie die Gelegenheit bieten, einem anderen Spieler zuzuhören. Außerdem helfen sie, den Takt zu halten sowie die Intonation und den Klang zu verbessern. Die letzten Stücke am Ende jedes Teils bieten die Gelegenheit, ein kurzes Stück mit Klavierbegleitung vom Blatt zu spielen.

**Teil 1** enthält die Noten C, E und G, wobei entweder mit C oder G begonnen werden kann, sowie einfache Rhythmen und Taktarten.

**Teil 2** enthält die Noten C bis G, hauptsächlich in Ganztonschritten und mit Tonwiederholungen. Taktarten: 4/4 und 2/4.

**Teil 3** enthält dieselben fünf Noten und zusätzlich das Fis sowie die Tonart G-Dur. Der 3/4-Takt wird in Verbindung mit der punktierten Halben und der punktierten Viertel eingeführt.

**In Teil 4** wird der Tonumfang auf die Oktave C–C erweitert, und es werden das B, F-Dur, Achtel und weitere punktierte Rhythmen eingeführt.

**In Teil 5** wird der Tonumfang um Es und F erweitert sowie die neuen Tonarten D-, Es-, A- und B-Dur eingeführt. Außerdem kommen der 3/8- und 6/8-Takt sowie gebundene Achtel hinzu.

**Teil 6** beginnt mit Stücken in zusammengesetzten Taktarten und enthält weitere Molltonarten sowie Des-Dur. Sechzehntel in einfachen Taktarten, Bindebogen und Triolen werden verwendet, und der Tonumfang wird erweitert. Außerdem werden sowohl dynamische Zeichen als auch Vortragsangaben eingeführt.

**In Teil 7** geht es hauptsächlich um swingende Achtel und Triolenfiguren.

**Teil 8** vereint verschiedene Stilrichtungen, Tonarten und Rhythmen, die zuvor eingeführt wurden.

**Teil 9** enthält einfache Transpositionen, d.h. man spielt einen Ganzton höher oder tiefer. Es folgen einige chromatische und modale Beispiele sowie Stücke im 5/4- und 5/8-Takt.

**Teil 10** beginnt mit weiteren Übungen zum Transponieren und enthält einige Tanzstile, die Ganztonleiter sowie die Taktarten 7/4 und 7/8.

**Teil 11** enthält alle Tonarten, Doppelkreuze und -Bes, einige Stilrichtungen von Barock bis zur atonalen Musik sowie den gesamten erweiterten Tonumfang.

## An den Schüler: Warum Vom-Blatt-Spiel?

Abgesehen davon, dass einige Prüfungsgremien eine Prüfung im Vom-Blatt-Spiel verlangen, hilft dir niemand, wenn du zu Hause, im Unterricht oder bei einem Vorspiel ein neues Stück spielen willst – nur du selbst! Die Fähigkeit, Taktart und Noten korrekt zu lesen und die Phrasierung und Dynamik schnell zu erfassen, ist wahrscheinlich das Wichtigste, was du erlernen kannst.

Ziel dieses Buches ist es, dir beim Selbstunterricht behilflich zu sein. Das Buch zeigt dir, worauf du achten sollst und wie du dich in sehr kurzer Zeit am besten vorbereitest. Das tust du, indem du dir Takt- und Tonart sowie den Verlauf der Melodie und die Ausdruckszeichen genau anschaust. Die kurzen Musikstücke steigern sich nur allmählich, um sowohl dein Vertrauen und deine Beobachtungsgabe aufzubauen als auch, um dich dazu zu befähigen, exakt vom Blatt zu spielen. Am Ende jeden Teils stehen Duette, die du mit deinem Lehrer oder deinen Freunden spielen kannst. Außerdem gibt es Stücke mit Klavierbegleitung, die deine Fähigkeit im Blatt-Spiel überprüfen, während gleichzeitig etwas anderes abläuft. Das ist eine wesentliche Fähigkeit, wenn man mit einer Band, einem Orchester oder einer anderen Musikgruppe zusammenspielt.

Wenn du jedes Mal, wenn du trompete spielst, auch etwas vom Blatt spielst, wirst du überrascht sein, wie sehr du dich verbesserst. Denke daran: wenn du die meisten Melodien, die du spielen sollst, vom Blatt spielen kannst, kannst du dich auf die „schwierigen Teile" konzentrieren und diese viel schneller beherrschen.

Stelle dir die Melodien in diesem Buch als „Ministücke" vor und versuche, sie schnell und korrekt zu lernen. Wenn du dann wirklich vom Blatt spielen musst, wirst du bestens ausgerüstet sein, um gleich beim ersten Versuch erfolgreich zu sein.

*Jetzt bist du auf dich selbst gestellt!*

# Section 1 – Introducing notes C, E and G

## Section 1 – Introduction des notes *do, mi* et *sol*

## *Teil 1 – Die Noten C, E und G*

In this initial section you will be asked to read just 3 notes, C, E and G in the key of C major using 1 beat, 2 beat and 4 beat note values.

**General tips**
**Always look at the rhythm first.** You should tap, clap or sing the rhythm before you play any notes. By doing this you will not only have looked at every note but also see if there is a pattern in either the rhythm or the shape of the melody.

**Always try to keep going.** This is easier if you choose a sustainable tempo and also give yourself at least one bar of counting before you begin.

Dans cette première partie, il ne vous sera demandé de lire que trois notes, *do, mi* et *sol*, dans la tonalité de *do* majeur, en utilisant des valeurs de notes de un, deux et quatre temps.

**Indications générales**
**Toujours étudier le rythme en premier.** À vous de le frapper, de le taper dans les mains ou de le battre avant de jouer les notes. Ce faisant, vous aurez non seulement eu chaque note sous les yeux, mais cela vous aura également permis d'identifier un éventuel motif rythmique ou mélodique.

**Essayer d'aller de l'avant sans vous arrêter.** Cela vous sera plus facile si vous choisissez un tempo raisonnable et comptez une mesure avant de commencer.

Im ersten Teil musst du nur drei Noten lesen: C, E und G in der Tonart C-Dur. Die Notendauer beträgt entweder einen Schlag, zwei Schläge oder vier Schläge.

**Allgemeine Tipps**
**Sieh dir immer zuerst den Rhythmus an.** Du solltest den Rhythmus klatschen, mit dem Fuß klopfen oder singen, bevor du die Noten spielst. Auf diese Weise schaust du dir nicht nur jede einzelne Note an, sondern siehst auch, ob es im Rhythmus oder Melodieverlauf ein Muster gibt.

**Du solltest versuchen, immer weiterzuspielen.** Das ist einfacher, wenn du ein gleich bleibendes Tempo wählst und mindestens einen Takt einzählst, bevor du anfängst.

# Section 1 – Introducing notes C, E and G

Section 1 – Introduction des notes *do*, *mi* et *sol*

*Teil 1 – Die Noten C, E und G*

New note: C                          Nouvelle note : *do*                        Neue Note: C

Alternative starting note G               *Sol* note de départ alternative             Alternativer Anfangston G

**6.**

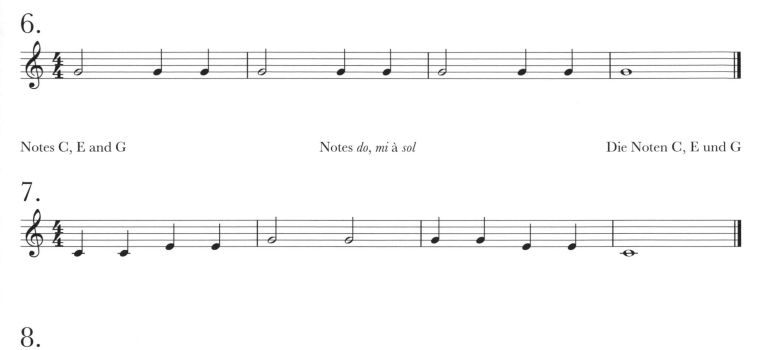

Notes C, E and G          Notes *do, mi* à *sol*          Die Noten C, E und G

**7.**

**8.**

**9.**

**10.**

Note against note          Note contre note          Erstes Zusammenspiel

**11.**

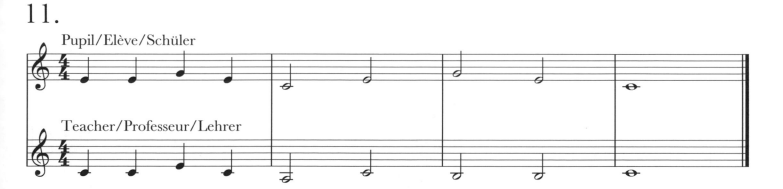

Pupil/Elève/Schüler

Teacher/Professeur/Lehrer

**12.**

**13.**

**In march style**

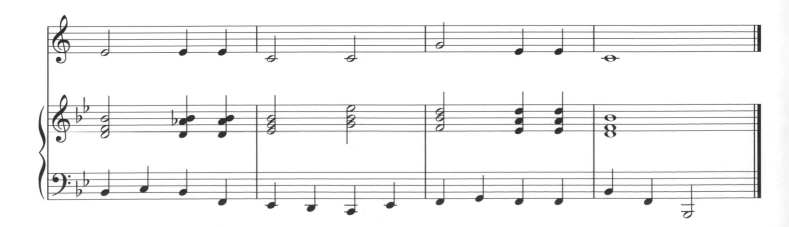

# Section 2 – Notes C-G, 2/4 time
## Section 2 – Notes *do* à *sol*, mesure à 2/4
### *Teil 2 – Die Noten C-G, 2/4-Takt*

You now have 5 notes to play from C to G in either 2 or 4-time.

**General tips**
**Always look at the rhythm first.** You should tap, clap or sing the rhythm before you play any notes.

**Look at the shape of the notes.** Notice where the melody rises and falls and also **notice the movement.** Do the notes move by step or miss out a note (skip)? Be on the lookout for **repeated notes** too.

**Always try to keep a steady unbroken beat or pulse.**

Cette fois, vous avez cinq notes à jouer, de *do* à *sol*, dans des mesures à 2 ou 4 temps.

**Indications générales**
**Commencez toujours par regarder le rythme,** que vous taperez, frapperez dans les mains ou battrez avant de jouer une note.

**Observez la ligne des notes.** Repérez les mouvements ascendants et descendants de la mélodie ainsi que leur nature : s'agit-il de **mouvements** conjoints ou disjoints ? Soyez également attentif aux **notes répétées.**

**Tentez toujours de conserver une pulsation stable et régulière.**

Jetzt musst du fünf Noten spielen: von C bis G, entweder im Zweier- oder Vierertakt.

**Allgemeine Tipps**
**Sieh dir immer zuerst den Rhythmus an.** Du solltest den Rhythmus klatschen, mit dem Fuß klopfen oder singen, bevor du die Noten spielst.

**Sieh dir die Form der Noten an.** Achte darauf, wo die Melodie steigt und fällt und **beachte auch die Intervalle.** Bewegen sich die Noten in Ganztonschritten, oder wird eine Note ausgelassen (übersprungen)? Außerdem solltest du auf **Tonwiederholungen** achten.

**Probiere immer, einen ganz gleichmäßigen Beat bzw. Puls beizubehalten.**

# Section 2 – Notes C-G, 2/4 time

Section 2 – Notes *do* à *sol*, mesure à 2/4

*Teil 2 – Die Noten C-G, 2/4-Takt*

14.

15.

16.

**17.**

**18.**

**19.**

Pupil/Elève/Schüler

Teacher/Professeur/Lehrer

**20.**

**21.**

**Moderato**

# Section 3 – Introducing G major and F♯

## Section 3 – Introduction de *sol* majeur et du *fa*♯

## *Teil 3 – G-Dur und Fis*

This section introduces a number of new features.
The note: F♯.
3-time and the 3 beat dotted minim.
A dotted rhythm in 3/4 time.

**General tips**
**Make sure you check the time signature and work out the rhythm first.** This is most important now that a new time signature and further variation in the rhythms have been added.

**Look for the key signature.**
Pieces may be in C major or G major, and you may be required to **remember** where the F♯'s are to be played.

**Look for the rise and fall of the melody** and be prepared for changes of direction, repeated notes and movement by step, skip or larger intervals.

**Always try to keep a steady unbroken beat or pulse.**

Cette section introduit un certain nombre de nouveaux éléments :
La note *fa*♯,
La mesure ternaire et les blanches pointées sur trois temps,
Le rythme pointé dans une mesure à 3/4.

**Indications générales**
**Assurez-vous d'avoir vérifié la mesure et commencez par travailler le rythme.** Il s'agit d'un point d'autant plus important qu'une nouvelle mesure et des variations rythmiques supplémentaires ont été ajoutées.

**Repérez la tonalité.** Les pièces peuvent être en *do* ou en *sol* majeur et vous aurez peut-être besoin de **vous rappeler** où les *fa*♯ doivent être joués.

**Repérez les mouvements ascendants et descendants de la mélodie.** Et préparez-vous aux changements de direction, aux notes répétées et à la nature des mouvements, conjoints ou disjoints, avec de grands ou de petits intervalles.

**Essayez toujours de conserver une pulsation stable et régulière.**

In diesem Teil werden einige neue Aspekte vorgestellt:
die Note Fis,
der Dreiertakt und die punktierte Halbe, die drei Schläge zählt,
ein punktierter Rhythmus im 3/4-Takt.

**Allgemeine Tipps**
**Schau dir zuerst die Taktart und den Rhythmus an.** Das ist jetzt besonders wichtig, da eine neue Taktart und weitere rhythmische Variationen hinzukommen.

**Beachte die Tonart.** Die Stücke können in C-Dur oder G-Dur stehen, d.h. du solltest wissen, wann du Fis statt F spielen musst.

**Achte auf den Melodieverlauf** und bereite dich auf Richtungswechsel, Tonwiederholungen und Bewegungen in Tonschritten, Sprüngen oder größeren Intervallen vor.

**Versuche, durchgängig den Takt zu halten.**

16

# Section 3 – Introducing G major and F#

Section 3 – Introduction de *sol* majeur et du *fa*#

*Teil 3 – G-Dur und Fis*

C major                                                    *do* majeur                                                    C-Dur

22.

New note: F#                                          Nouvelle note : *fa*#                                          Neue note: Fis

23.

G major                                                    *sol* majeur                                                    G-Dur

24.

25.

Introducing 3/4 time and the dotted minim

Introduction de la mesure à 3 temps et de la blanche pointée

Einführung des 3/4-Taktes und der punktierten halben Note

18

**31.**

C major                              *do* majeur                              C-Dur

**32.**

Pupil/Elève/Schüler

Teacher/Professeur/Lehrer

G major                              *sol* majeur                              G-Dur

**33.**

34.

35.

# Section 4 – Notes C-C, incl. F♯ and B♭, 3-time, quavers and dotted rhythms

## Section 4 – Notes de *do* à *do*, y compris *fa♯* et *si♭*, mesure à 3 temps, croches et rythmes pointés

## *Teil 4 – Die Noten C-C einschl. Fis und B Dreiertakt, Achtel und punktierte Rhythmen*

Your range of notes now extends to an octave and includes both the **F♯** and a new note, **B♭**. You will also find pairs of quavers as well as the dotted rhythm used in Section 3.

**General tips**
**Always work through the rhythm thoroughly before you play.** Some of the pieces begin on the last beat of the bar in either 3 or 4-time, so it is even more important that you **count yourself in.** Always choose a tempo that you will be able to sustain.

**Your key signature may contain either one sharp (G major) or one flat (F major).** Remember that the **key signature** is the **only reminder** that you are required to play the accidental that is right for that key.

**Take a good look at the shape and movement** as this will not be restricted to just steps and skips. You will find a number of **intervals** including 4ths, 5ths and 6ths.

**Always try to keep a steady unbroken beat or pulse.**

L'étendue de vos notes est maintenant d'une octave et comprend à la fois le *fa♯* et une nouvelle note, le *si♭*. Vous rencontrerez aussi des croches par deux ainsi que le rythme pointé utilisé dans la section 3.

**Indications générales**
**Travaillez toujours soigneusement le rythme avant de jouer.** Certaines des pièces commencent sur le dernier temps d'une mesure à 3 ou 4 temps, ainsi est-il d'autant plus important que vous vous mettiez dans le rythme. Choisissez toujours un tempo que vous serez capable de maintenir.

**La tonalité comprendra peut-être un dièse (*sol* majeur) ou un bémol (*fa* majeur).** Souvenez-vous que l'**armure** et le **seul moyen de vous rappeler** que vous devez jouer les altérations propres à cette tonalité.

**Observez attentivement la ligne et le mouvement** de la mélodie, car il ne se réduira pas uniquement à des mouvements conjoints ou à de petits intervalles. Vous trouverez également un certain nombre d'**intervalles** incluant quartes, quintes et sixtes.

**Essayez toujours de conserver une pulsation stable et régulière.**

Dein Notenumfang wird jetzt auf eine Oktave erweitert und enthält sowohl das **Fis** als auch die neue Note **B**. Außerdem findest du Achtelpaare sowie den punktierten Rhythmus aus Teil 3.

**Allgemeine Tipps**
**Schau dir vor dem Spielen immer zuerst den Rhythmus genau an.** Einige Stücke beginnen auf dem letzten Taktschlag und stehen entweder im Dreier oder Viertakt. Daher ist es umso wichtiger, dass du **einzählst.** Wähle immer ein Tempo, das du auch halten kannst.

**Die Tonart kann entweder ein Kreuz (G-Dur) oder ein Be (F-Dur) enthalten.** Denk daran, dass die **Tonartvorzeichnung** der **einzige Hinweis** darauf ist, dass du das Vorzeichen der jeweiligen Tonart beachten musst.

**Sieh dir Melodieverlauf und -bewegung genau an,** da sich diese nicht auf Tonschritte und Sprünge beschränken. Du wirst auch zahlreiche **Intervalle** finden, z.B. Quarten, Quinten und Sexten.

**Versuche, durchgängig den Takt zu halten.**

# Section 4 – Notes C-C, incl. F♯ and B♭, 3-time, quavers and dotted rhythms

Section 4 – Notes de *do* à *do*, y compris *fa*♯ et *si*♭, mesure à 3 temps, croches et rythmes pointés

*Teil 4 – Die Noten C-C einschl. Fis und B Dreiertakt, Achtel und punktierte Rhythmen*

C major · *do* majeur · C-Dur

Introducing quavers (eighth notes) · Introduction des croches · Einführung von Achteln

G major · *sol* majeur · G-Dur

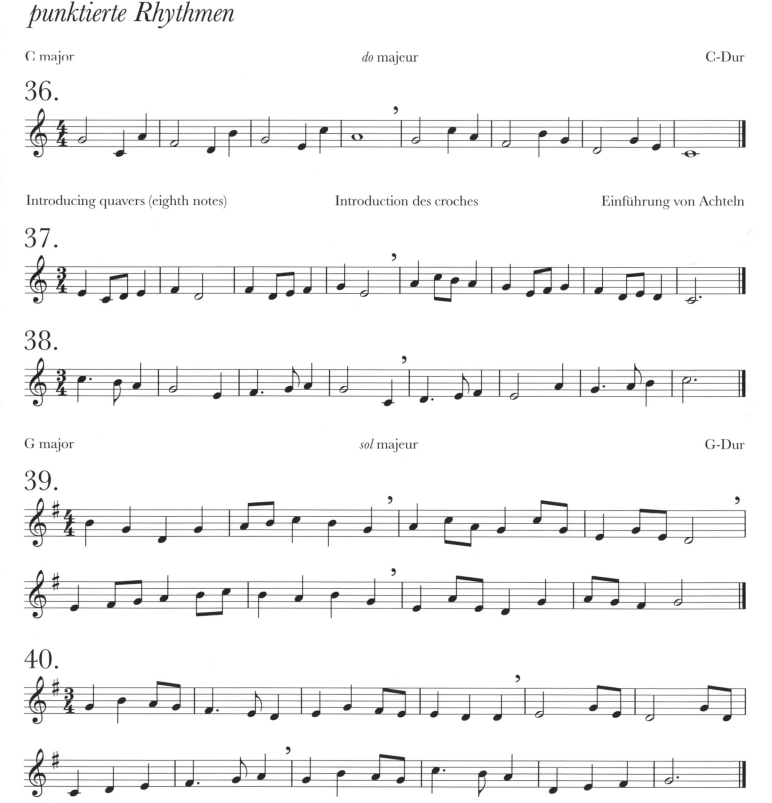

22

This begins on the 3rd beat of the bar in 3-time. Count 1 2 3 1 2 before you begin

Cette pièce débute sur le 3e temps d'une mesure à 3 temps. Comptez 1, 2, 3, 1, 2, avant de commencer

Dieses Stück beginnt auf dem dritten Schlag in einem 3/4-Takt. Zähle 1 2 3 1 2 vor, bevor du anfängst

**41.**

F major          *fa* majeur          F-Dur

**42.**

**43.**

This begins on the 4th beat of the bar in 4-time. Count 1 2 3 before you begin

Cette pièce débute sur le 4e temps d'une mesure à 4 temps. Comptez 1, 2, 3, avant de commencer

Dieses Stück beginnt auf dem vierten Schlag in einem 4/4-Takt. Zähle 1 2 3 vor, bevor du anfängst

**44.**

This begins on the 3rd beat of the bar in 3-time. Count 1 2 3 1 2 before you begin

Cette pièce débute sur le 3e temps d'une mesure à 3 temps. Comptez 1, 2, 3, 1, 2, avant de commencer

Dieses Stück beginnt auf dem dritten Schlag in einem 3/4-Takt. Zähle 1 2 3 1 2 vor, bevor du anfängst

**45.**

Both parts may be played by the pupil or pupils. This begins on the 4th beat in 4-time. Count one whole bar, then 1 2 breath (on 3) before you begin.
C major

Les deux partiès peuvent être janées par l'elève ou par deux elèves. Cette pièce débute sur le 4e temps d'une mesure à 4 temps. Comptez une mesure entière, ensuite 1, 2, inspirer (sur 3) avant de commencer.
*do* majeur

Beide Stimmen können von Schüler und lehrer oder von zwei Schülern gespielt werden. Dieses Stück beginnt auf dem vierten Schlag in einem 4/4-Takt. Zähle einen ganzen Takt, dann 1 2 atmen (auf der 3), bevor du anfängst.
C-Dur

**46.**

G major          *sol* majeur          G-Dur

**47.**

This begins on the 3rd beat of the bar in 3-time. Count one whole bar, then 1 breath (on 2) before you begin.
F major

Cette pièce débute sur le 3e temps d'une mesure à 3 temps. Comptez une mesure entière, ensuite 1, inspirer (sur 2) avant de commencer.
*fa* majeur

Dieses Stück beginnt auf dem dritten Schlag in einem 3/4-Takt. Zähle einen ganzen Takt, dann 1 atmen (auf der 2), bevor du anfängst.
F-Dur

**48.**

G major                                       *sol* majeur                                       G-Dur

**49.**

F major                                       *fa* majeur                                       F-Dur

**50.**

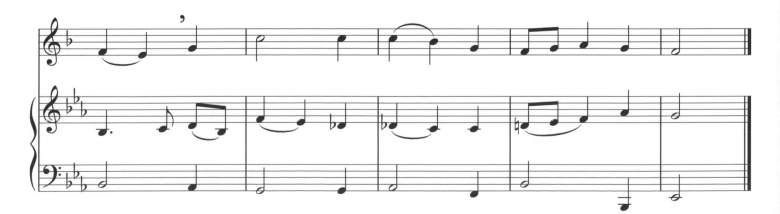

# Section 5 – Keys D, A, E♭ and B♭ majors, D minor, 3/8 and 6/8 time, dynamic marks: *p, mf, f*

## Section 5 – Tonalités de *ré, la, mi*♭ et *si*♭ majeur, *ré* mineur, mesures à 3/8 et 6/8, indications de nuances : *p, mf, f*

## Teil 5 – Tonarten: D-, A-, Es u. B-Dur, d-Moll, 3/8- und 6/8-Takt, dynamische Zeichen: *p, mf, f*

In this section the range of notes, keys and rhythms is further extended, introducing 6/8 time signatures and slurs for some quaver pairs.
Range: from C to E♭.
New keys:  D and A major.
B♭ and E♭ majors.
D minor

**Basic Dynamic markings introduced.**

*p*    Quiet, gentle.

*mf*   Fairly loud.

*f*    Loud, strong.

**Never start to play until you have understood the rhythms** and have chosen a suitable tempo. You may need to do this 3 or 4 times before you are ready to play.

**With so many new keys** it is vital that you find the sharps or flats you need to play and to know where they are in the piece. A good knowledge of the scales will make this easier.

**Be on the lookout for patterns.** Most tunes have some form of repetition in either the rhythms used or in the shape of the melody or in its movement. A **sequence** is a repeated pattern that moves either up or down. See if you notice any as they may help when you are playing.

**Always try to keep a steady unbroken beat or pulse.**

Dans cette partie, la palette des notes, des tonalités et des rythmes est encore enrichie, avec l'introduction de mesures à 6/8 ainsi que de liaisons par deux entre les croches.
Étendue : de *do* à *mi*♭.
Nouvelles tonalités :
*ré* et *la* majeur
*si* bémol et *mi* bémol majeur
*ré* mineur.

**Introduction des indications dynamiques de base**

*p*    calme, doux.

*mf*   assez fort.

*f*    fort, puissant.

**Ne commencez jamais à jouer avant d'avoir compris les rythmes** et choisi un tempo adapté. Vous aurez peut-être besoin de trois à quatre lectures avant d'être prêt(e) à jouer.

**Avec autant de nouvelles tonalités,** il est vital que vous repériez les dièses et les bémols à jouer et que vous sachiez où ils se situent dans le morceau. Une bonne connaissance des gammes vous facilitera la tâche.

**Soyez attentif aux motifs.** La plupart des airs présentent des formes de répétitions, soit dans les rythmes utilisés soit dans la ligne mélodique ou dans son mouvement. Une **séquence** est un motif répété, ascendant ou descendant. Voyez si vous en décelez certaines, car elles vous aideront dans votre jeu.

**Essayez toujours de garder une pulsation stable et régulière.**

In diesem Teil wird der Umfang der Noten, Tonarten und Rhythmen nochmals erweitert. Hier lernst du den 6/8-Takt und den Bindebogen für Achtelpaare kennen.
Umfang: von C bis Es
Neue Tonarten:    D- und A-Dur
B- und Es-Dur
d-Moll

**Einführung wichtiger dynamischer Zeichen:**

*p*    leise, sanft.

*mf*   mittellaut.

*f*    laut, kräftig.

**Fang erst an zu spielen, wenn du die Rhythmen verstanden** und ein angemessenes Tempo gefunden hast. Es kann sein, dass du dich drei- oder viermal damit beschäftigen musst, bevor du spielen kannst.

**Bei vielen neuen Tonarten** musst du zuerst die Kreuze und Bes finden, die du spielen musst und wissen, wo im Stück sie sich befinden. Gute Tonleiterkenntnisse erleichtern diese Aufgabe.

**Halte nach Mustern (Patterns) Ausschau.** Die meisten Stücke enthalten entweder im Rhythmus oder im Melodieverlauf Wiederholungen. Eine **Sequenz** ist ein wiederholtes Pattern, das entweder steigt oder fällt.

**Versuche, durchgängig den Takt zu halten.**

# Section 5 – Keys D, A, E♭ and B♭ majors, D minor, 3/8 and 6/8 time, dynamic marks: *p, mf, f*

Section 5 – Tonalités de *ré, la, mi♭* et *si♭* majeur, *ré* mineur, mesures à 3/8 et 6/8, indications de nuances : *p, mf, f*

*Teil 5 – Tonarten: D-, A-, Es u. B-Dur, d-Moll, 3/8- und 6/8-Takt, dynamische Zeichen: p, mf, f*

This begins on the 3rd beat of the bar in 4-time. Count 1 2 3 4 1 2 before you begin

Cette pièce débute sur le 3e temps d'une mesure à 4 temps. Comptez 1, 2, 3, 4, 1, 2, avant de commencer

Dieses Stück beginnt auf dem dritten Schlag in einem 4/4-Takt. Zähle 1 2 3 4 1 2 vor, bevor du anfängst

### 51.

### 52.

New key: D major

Nouvelle tonalité : *ré* majeur

Neue Tonart: D-Dur

### 53.

This begins on the 4th beat of the bar in 4-time. Count 1 2 3 before you begin (breathe on the final '3')

Cette pièce débute sur le 4e temps d'une mesure à 4 temps. Comptez 1, 2, 3, avant de commencer (respirez sur le "3" final)

Dieses Stück beginnt auf dem vierten Schlag in einem 4/4-Takt. Zähle 1 2 3 vor, bevor du anfängst (atme auf der letzten „3")

### 54.

This begins on the 3rd beat of the bar in 3-time. Count 1 2 3 1 2 before you begin

Cette pièce débute sur le 3e temps d'une mesure à 3 temps. Comptez 1, 2, 3, 1, 2, avant de commencer

Dieses Stück beginnt auf dem dritten Schlag in einem 3/4-Takt. Zähle 1 2 3 1 2 vor, bevor du anfängst

**55.**

This begins on the 3rd beat of the bar in 3-time. Count 1 2 3 1 2 before you begin.

Cette pièce débute sur le 3e temps d'une mesure à 3 temps. Comptez 1, 2, 3, 1, 2, avant de commencer.

Dieses Stück beginnt auf dem dritten Schlag in einem 3/4-Takt. Zähle 1 2 3 1 2 vor, bevor du anfängst.

D minor

*ré* mineur

d-Moll

**56.**

New key: A major

Nouvelle tonalité : *la* majeur

Neue Tonart: A-Dur

**57.**

**58.**

New key: B♭ major

Nouvelle tonalité : *si*♭ majeur

Neue Tonart: B-Dur

**59.**

**60.**

Introducing 3/8 time

Mesure à 3/8

3/8-Takt

**61.**

**62.**

New key: E♭ major

Nouvelle tonalité : *mi*♭ majeur

Neue Tonart: Es-Dur

**63.**

**64.**

Introducing 6/8 time

Mesure à 6/8

6/8-Takt

**65.**

**66.**

**67.**

**68.**

This begins on the 4th beat of the bar in 4-time. Count one whole bar, then count 1 2 breathe (on 3) before you begin

Cette pièce débute sur le 4e temps d'une mesure à 4 temps. Comptez une mesure entière, ensuite 1, 2, inspirer (sur 3) avant de commencer

Dieses Stück beginnt auf dem vierten Schlag in einem 4/4-Takt. Zähle einen ganzen Takt, dann 1 2 atme (auf der 3), bevor du anfängst

**69.**

**70.**

**71.**

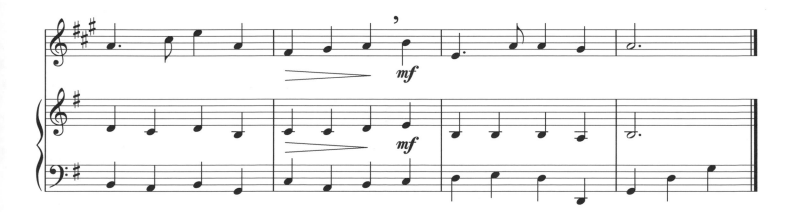

72.

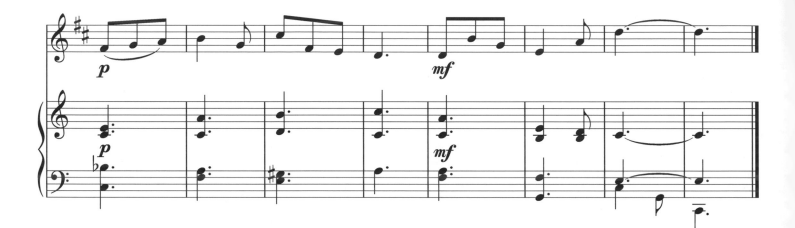

73.

# Section 6 – Range: B♭-G. Keys: A, D, G, C and F minor, D♭ major. New features: Compound time, semiquavers and triplets. Performance directions and dynamics

Section 6 – Étendue de *si♭* à *sol*. Tonalités : *la, ré, sol, do* et *fa* mineur, *ré* bémol majeur. Nouveaux éléments : mesures ternaires, doubles croches et triolets. Indications de jeu et de nuances

*Teil 6 – Umfang: B-G. Tonarten: a-, d-, g-, c- und f-Moll, Des-Dur. Neue Aspekte: Zusammengesetzte Taktarten, Sechzehntel u. Triolen. Vortragsangaben u. Dynamik*

The main features of this section are a continuation of Compound Time with 6/8 and 9/8 time signatures, the use of semiquavers and triplets and a number of new keys. These are clearly introduced at the start of each piece.

**With so many new rhythms and time values** it is vital that you master the rhythms of each piece before you play.

**Always** consider the rhythms first.
**Always** be aware of the key and tonality of each piece.
**Always** look out for sequences or other repeated features and patterns that make reading much easier.
**Always** set a suitable pulse and attempt to maintain it.

La poursuite de la découverte des mesures composées à 6/8 et à 9/8, l'utilisation des doubles croches et des triolets et quelques nouvelles tonalités constituent les éléments principaux de cette section. Ceux-ci sont clairement présentés au début de chaque morceau.

**Avec autant de nouveaux rythmes et de mesures,** il est vital que vous maîtrisiez les rythmes de chaque pièce avant de jouer.

Occupez vous **toujours** du rythme avant toute chose.
Ayez **toujours** conscience de la tonalité de chaque morceau.
Soyez **toujours** attentif aux séquences et à tout autre élément ou motif répétitif susceptible de faciliter la lecture.
Adoptez **toujours** une pulsation adaptée et essayez de la maintenir.

Die Hauptaspekte in Teil 6 sind die Fortsetzung der zusammengesetzten Taktarten 6/8 und 9/8, die Verwendung von Sechzehnteln und Triolen sowie einige neue Tonarten. Diese werden zu Beginn jedes Stückes vorgestellt.

**Angesichts so vieler neuer Rhythmen und Notenwerte** ist es wichtig, dass du dich mit den Rhythmen jedes Stückes vertraut machst, bevor du es spielst.

Sieh dir **immer** zuerst die Rhythmen an.
Du solltest **immer** die Tonart und den Grundton des jeweiligen Stückes kennen.
Achte **immer** auf Sequenzen oder andere Wiederholungen und Patterns, die das Vom-Blatt-Spiel erleichtern.
Versuche, **immer** gleichmäßig zu spielen und den Takt zu halten.

*Performance directions used in this section.*

*Indications de jeu utilisées dans cette section :*

*Vortragsangaben, die in Teil 6 verwendet werden:*

| | | | |
|---|---|---|---|
| Andante | at a walking pace | allant | gehend |
| Andantino | a little faster than Andante | un peu plus vite qu'andante | ein bisschenschneller als Andante |
| Barcarolle | a Venetian boating song | chanson vénitienne de gondolier | venezianisches Gondellied |
| Con spiritoso | with spirit | avec esprit | mit Geist |
| Dolce | sweetly, gently | doux | süß |
| Maestoso | majestically | mejesteusement | majestätisch |
| Moderato | at a moderate speed | modéré | in gemäßigtem Tempo |
| Ritmico | rhythmically | rythmique | rhythmisch |
| Sostenuto | sustained | soutenu | verhalten, getragen |
| Poco rit. | a little slower | retenu | zurückhaltend |
| Vivace | lively | vif | lebhaft |

# Section 6 – Range: B♭-G. Keys: A, D, G, C and F minor, D♭ major. New features: Compound time, semiquavers and triplets. Performance directions and dynamics

Section 6 – Étendue de *si♭* à *sol*. Tonalités : *la*, *ré*, *sol*, *do* et *fa* mineur, *ré* bémol majeur. Nouveaux éléments : mesures ternaires, doubles croches et triolets. Indications de jeu et de nuances

*Teil 6 – Umfang: B-G. Tonarten: a-, d-, g-, c- und f-Moll, Des-Dur. Neue Aspekte: Zusammengesetzte Taktarten, Sechzehntel u. Triolen. Vortragsangaben u. Dynamik*

**74.** **Con spirito**

| This piece begins on the last quaver in 6/8 time. Count 1 (2 3)  1 (2 3) before you begin.<br><br>New key: G minor | Cette pièce commence sur la dernière croche d'une mesure à 6/8. Comptez mentalement 1 (2 3)  1 (2 3) avant d'attaquer.<br><br>Nouvelle tonalité : *sol* mineur | Dieses Stück beginnt auf dem letzten Achtel in einem 6/8-Takt. Zähle 1 (2 3)  1 (2 3) bevor du anfängst.<br><br>Neue Tonart: g-Moll |

**75.** **Moderato**

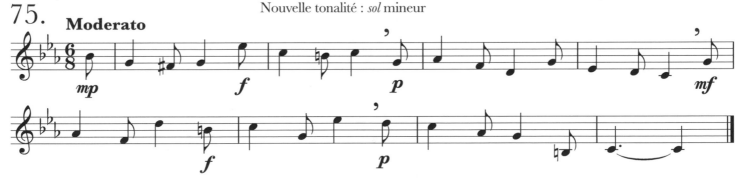

| This piece begins on the last quaver in 6/8 time. Count 1 (2 3)  1 (2 3) before you begin | Cette pièce commence sur la dernière croche d'une mesure à 6/8. Comptez mentalement 1 (2 3)  1 (2 3) avant d'attaquer | Dieses Stück beginnt auf dem letzten Achtel in einem 6/8-Takt. Zähle 1 (2 3)  1 (2 3) bevor du anfängst |

**76.** **Andante**

New time: 9/8
New key: D♭ major

Nouvelle mesure à 9/8
Nouvelle tonalité : *ré* bémol majeur

Neue Taktart: 9/8
Neue Tonart: Des-Dur

**77.**

Introducing semiquavers and triplets

Introduction des doubles croches et triolets

Einführung von Sechzehntel a. Triolen

**78.**

**79.**

**80.**

34

New key: F minor    Nouvelle tonalité : *fa* mineur    Neue Tonart: f-Moll

**81.** **Cantabile**

Count 1 2 3 1 2 before you begin    Comptez 1, 2, 3, 1, 2, avant de commencer    Zähle 1 2 3 1 2 vor, bevor du anfängst

**82.** **Ritmico**

**83.** **Maestoso**

**84.** **Con moto**

**poco rit.**

New key: A minor | Nouvelle tonalité : *la* mineur | Neue Tonart: a-Moll

## 85.

**Dolce**

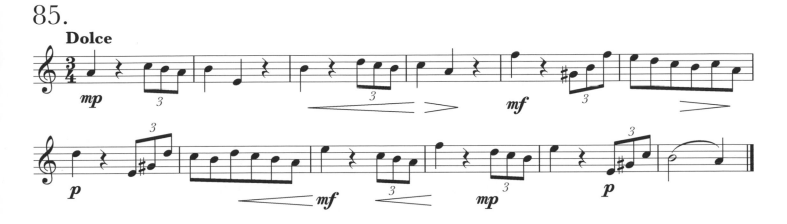

New key: F# minor | Nouvelle tonalité : *fa*# mineur | Neue Tonart: fis-Moll

## 86.

**Moderato**

## 87.

**Vivace**

**88.**

**Ritmico**

**89.**

**Andante cantabile**

**90.**

**Barcarolle**

poco rall.

# Section 7 – Swing style
## Section 7 – Le swing
### *Teil 7 – Swing-Stil*

All the pieces in this section are in *swing time*. That means that written quavers ♫ are to be played as ♪³♪ throughout. The note **on** the beat is always **longer** than the note **off** the beat.

**Essential features** to bear in mind when playing swing.

1. **Always count yourself in.** Traditionally a 'swing' count is: aOne - aTwo - aOne Two Three Four.

2. **Make sure you know the rhythm.** Most jazz players prefer to 'vocalise' the rhythms. By doing this you can differentiate between accented and staccato phrasing, and achieve a more authentic and stylistic syncopation and feel for the swing.

3. **Style** is all important. To achieve an authentic jazz feel, the staccato dot should be light and unaccented – rather like striking a closed high-hat cymbal. Any notes tied you can 'lean on' slightly and this is helped if the previous note is lightly shortened. When a phrase **ends** with a staccato, make it very short but never accented or clipped.

Tous les morceaux de cette partie sont swingués. Cela signifie que les croches écrites ♫ doivent être jouées comme ♪³♪ tout au long de la pièce. La note **sur** le temps est toujours plus **longue** que la note **faible**.

**Points essentiels** à garder à l'esprit lorsque l'on joue du swing.

1. **Mettez-vous toujours dans le rythme.** La manière traditionnelle de compter le swing est la suivante : aOne - aTwo - aOne Two Three Four.

2. **Assurez-vous de connaître le rythme.** La plupart des jazzmen préfère « **vocaliser** » les rythmes. Ce faisant, vous pourrez différencier les phrasés staccato et accentués et réaliser des syncopes plus authentiques et dans le style, pour une sensation de swing réussie.

3. **Le style** est particulièrement important. Pour parvenir à une authentique sensation jazz, le staccato sera léger et non accentué – comme lorsqu'on frappe une cymbale charleston fermée. Vous pouvez vous « appuyer » légèrement sur les notes liées, ce qui sera plus facile si la note précédente est légèrement écourtée. Lorsqu'une phrase se **termine** par un staccato, ce dernier doit être bref, mais jamais accentué ni précipité.

Alle Stücke in Teil 7 werden swingend gespielt. Das bedeutet, dass die notierten Achtel ♫ durchgängig wie folgt gespielt werden: ♪³♪ Die Note **auf der Zählzeit** ist immer **länger** als die Note auf dem „**und**".

**Wichtige Aspekte**, die beim Spielen von Swing-Achteln zu berücksichtigen sind:

1. **Zähle immer ein.** Meist werden Swing-Achtel folgendermaßen eingezählt: „eEins – eZwei – eEins – Zwei – Drei – Vier".

2. **Du solltest immer den Rhythmus kennen.** Die meisten Jazzmusiker „**vokalisieren**" die Rhythmen. Dadurch kann man zwischen betonter und Staccato-Phrasierung unterscheiden und eine authentischere und stilistisch bessere Synkopierung und ein besseres Gespür für den Swing entwickeln.

3. Der **Stil** ist äußerst wichtig. Um ein authentisches Jazz-Feeling zu erzeugen, sollte der Staccato-Punkt leicht und unbetont sein – wie der Schlag auf eine geschlossene Hi-Hat. An alle gebundenen Noten kannst du dich ein bisschen „anlehnen". Dabei hilft es, die vorherige Note etwas kürzer zu spielen. Wenn eine Phrase mit einem Staccato **endet**, sollte es sehr kurz, aber nie betont oder abgehackt gespielt werden.

# Section 7 – Swing style

## Section 7 – Le swing

*Teil 7 – Swing-Stil*

40

**94.**

Lively

**95.**

Medium swing

**96.**

Bright swing

molto rall.

**97.**

**98.**

**99.**

**100.**

**101.**

**102.**

**Medium swing**

**103.**

**Medium swing**

**104.**

**105.**

106.

# Section 8 – General revision using keys up to 4 sharps and flats

Section 8 – Révision générale utilisant les tonalités comportant jusqu'à 4 dièses ou bémols

*Teil 8 – Wiederholung der Tonarten bis zu 4 Kreuzen und Bes*

All keys, time values, rhythms and features encountered so far are revised in this section.

**You will still need to:**
**Check both the key and the time signatures.**
**Choose your tempo** according to the performance direction and what you observe of the style, intricacy and the texture.
**Always count at least one bar** before you begin to scan the rhythm. Many instrumentalists like to use their fingers to enable them to do a 'dry-run' of the rhythms and valves required.
**Never start to play until** every note has been looked at. Scanning with your voice will also help develop your sense of pitch and assist in giving an accurate performance.

Dans cette partie, toutes les tonalités, valeurs de notes, rythmes et éléments rencontrés jusqu'à présent font l'objet d'une révision.

**Vous aurez toujours besoin de :**
**Vérifier la tonalité et la mesure.**
**Choisir votre tempo** en fonction des indications de jeu et de vos observations relatives au style, la complexité et la texture de la partition.
**Comptez toujours au moins une mesure** avant de commencer à lire le rythme. De nombreux instrumentistes aiment faire une lecture « à blanc » des rythmes et des pistons requis avec leurs doigts.
**Ne commencez jamais à jouer avant** d'avoir lu chaque note. Parcourir la partition en la chantant vous aidera aussi à développer votre sens de la justesse et à en donner une interprétation adéquate.

In Teil 8 werden alle bisherigen Tonarten, Notenwerte, Rhythmen und Aspekte wiederholt.

**Du solltest nach wie vor:**
**sowohl die Tonart als auch die Taktart beachten, dein Tempo** gemäß der Vortragsbezeichnung und deinem Eindruck von Stil, Schwierigkeit und Stimmführung festlegen.
**Mindestens einen Takt einzählen,** bevor du den Rhythmus überfliegst. Viele Musiker machen zuerst mit den Fingern einen „Probedurchgang", um sich die Rhythmen und erforderlichen Ventile einzuprägen.
**Erst spielen,** wenn du dir jede einzelne Note angeschaut hast. Das Stück kurz durchzusingen oder -summen trägt außerdem dazu bei, dass du die Töne besser triffst und präziser spielst.

*Performance directions used in this section.*

*Indications de jeu utilisées dans cette section :*

*Vortragsangaben, die in Teil 8 verwendet werden:*

| | | | |
|---|---|---|---|
| Adagio | slowly | lent | langsam |
| Allegretto | moderately fast but not as fast as Allegro | assez rapide qu'allegro | gemäßigt schnell |
| Andante | at walking pace | allant | gehend |
| Ballad | a song like, generally slow tempo | sorte de chant, en général de tempo lent | ein meist langsames Stück |
| Cantabile | in a singing style | chantant | gesanglich |
| Con moto | with movement | avec movement | mit Bewegung |
| Gigue | a lively dance in compound time | danse animée en ternaire | lebhafter Tanz in zusammengesetzten Taktarten |
| Maestoso | majestically | mejesteusement | majestätisch |
| Moderato | at a moderate speed | modéré | in gemäßigtem Tempo |
| Ragtime | a highly syncopated early jazz style | style de jazz syncopé | ein früher Jazzstil mit synkopierter Melodie |
| Ritmico | rhythmically | rythmique | rhythmisch |
| Vivo | quick, lively | vif, rapide | schnell, lebhaft |

# Section 8 – General revision using keys up to 4 sharps and flats

Section 8 – Révision générale utilisant les tonalités comportant jusqu'à 4 dièses ou bémols

*Teil 8 – Wiederholung der Tonarten bis zu 4 Kreuzen und Bes*

**107.**

**108.**

**109.**

Moderato

**110.**

Ritmico

**111.**

Cantabile

**112.**

**Gentle swing**

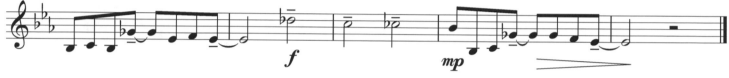

**113.**

**Medium swing**

**114.**

**Ragtime**

**115.**

**With sentimentality**

**116.**

**Vivo**

**117.**

**Gigue**

## 118.

## 119.

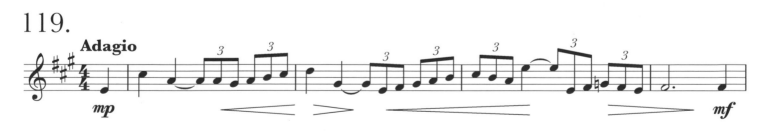

**120.**

Ritmico

poco rall.

**121.**

Ragtime

**122.**

**123.**

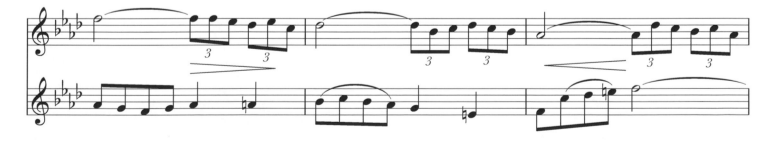

**124.**

**In a ballad style**

# Section 9 – Simple transposition, chromatic figures and Dorian mode, five-time – 5/4 and 5/8

Section 9 – Transposition simple, motifs chromatiques et mode dorien, mesures à cinq temps – 5/4 et 5/8

*Teil 9 – Einfache Transpositionen, chromatische Figuren und der dorische Modus, 5/4- u. 5/8-Takt*

In this section **transposition** is introduced. This entails playing a tune in a different key to that written by taking it either **up a tone** – as for Trumpet in C, or **down a tone** – as for Trumpet in A♭.
For further exercises in transposition you can use pieces from earlier sections.

Two new time signatures are employed, both in **five-time**.
Look to see if the 5 beats are divided as 2+3, or 3+2.
Both 5/4 and 5/8 are used.

Additions are made to the major and minor tonalities by the introduction of **chromatic phrases** and use of the **Dorian mode**.

*Performance directions used in this section.*

Cette partie introduit la **transposition**. Transposer signifie jouer un air dans une tonalité différente en **montant d'un ton** – comme pour la trompette en ut – ou en **descendant d'un ton**, comme pour la trompette en *la*♭. Vous pouvez utiliser les exercices des parties précédentes pour vous entraîner davantage à la transposition.

Deux nouvelles mesures sont employées, toutes deux à **cinq temps**. Vérifiez si les 5 temps sont subdivisés selon le modèle 2+3 ou 3+2. Utilisation à la fois de mesures à 5/4 et à 5/8.

Les tonalités majeures et mineures sont enrichies de **phrases chromatiques** et l'utilisation du **mode dorien**.

*Indications de jeu utilisées dans cette section :*

In diesem Teil lernst du das **Transponieren** kennen. Beim Transponieren wird ein Stück in einer anderen Tonart als der notierten gespielt, indem es entweder **einen Ton höher** – wie für Trompete in C, oder **einen Ton tiefer** – wie für Trompete in As gespielt wird.
Du kannst das Transponieren auch mit Stücken aus den vorherigen Abschnitten üben.

Zwei neue Taktarten kommen vor, beide sind **Fünfertakte**.
Finde heraus, ob die fünf Schläge in 2+3 oder 3+2 unterteilt sind.
Hier kommt sowohl der 5/4 als auch der 5/8-Takt vor.

Dur- und Molltonarten werden durch die Einführung **chromatischer Phrasen** und die Verwendung des **dorischen Modus** ergänzt.

*Vortragsangaben, die in Teil 9 verwendet werden:*

| | | | |
|---|---|---|---|
| Andante | at walking pace | allant | gehend |
| Con moto | with movement | avec movement | mit Bewegung |
| Dolce | sweetly, gently | doux | süß |
| Mesto | sadly | triste | traurig |
| Minuet | a stylish dance in 3-time from the Classical era | menuet – courte et majestueuse danse à trios temps | kurzes, majestätisches stück im 3/4-Takt |
| Risoluto | with resolve, purposefully | résolut | entschlossen |
| Waltz | a 3-time dance from the 19th Century | danse à trois temps du 19e siècle | tanz aus dem 19. jahrhundert im 3/4-Takt |

# Section 9 – Simple transposition, chromatic figures and Dorian mode, five-time – 5/4 and 5/8

Section 9 – Transposition simple, motifs chromatiques et mode dorien, mesures à cinq temps – 5/4 et 5/8

*Teil 9 – Einfache Transpositionen, chromatische Figuren und der dorische Modus, 5/4- u. 5/8-Takt*

Transpose: Trumpet in C
(transpose up a tone)

Transposez : trompette en *ut*
(transposez un ton au-dessus)

Transponieren: C-Trompete
(einen Ton aufwärts transponieren)

Transpose: Trumpet in A♭
(transpose down a tone)

Transposez : trompette en *la* bémol
(transposez un ton en dessous)

Transponieren: As-Trompete
(einen Ton abwärts transponieren)

Transpose down a tone

Tranposez un ton en dessous

Einen Ton abwärts transponieren

For additional pieces to transpose pieces in Sections 1-3 may be used

Pour davantage d'exercises de transposition, vous pouvez utiliser les pièces des Sections 1 à 3

Als weitere Stücke zum Transponieren können die Stücke in Teil 1-3 verwendet werden

Introducing 5-time.
This begins on the 5th beat in 5-time.
Count one whole bar, then 1 2 3 4

Introduction de la mesure à 5 temps.
Cette pièce d´bute sur le 5e temps
d'une mesure à 5 temps. Comptez
une mesure entière, ensuite 1, 2, 3, 4

Einführung des 5-Takt.
Dieses Stück beginnt auf dem fünften
Schlag in einem 5/4-Takt. Zähle
einen ganzen Takt, dann 1 2 3 4

**131.**

**In a flowing style**

**132.**

**Moderato**

**133.**

**Resoluto**

**134.**

**Con moto**

**135.**

**Dolce**

Introducing chromatic sequences    Introduction de séquences chromatiques    Einführung chromatischer sequenzen

## 136.

## 137.

## 138.

Dorian mode (in D)          Mode dorien (*ré*)          Dorische Modus (D)

## 139.

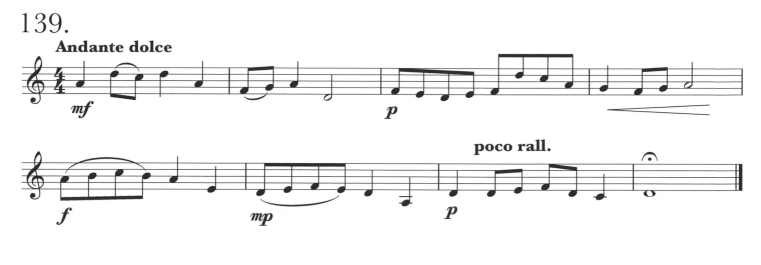

Pentatonic (E♭)          Gamme pentatonic (*mi♭*)          Pentatonische Tonleiter (Es)

## 140.

## 141.

**142.**

**143.**

**144.**

**Andante moderato**

**145.**

**Andante sostenuto**

**146.**

**In the style of a Minuet**

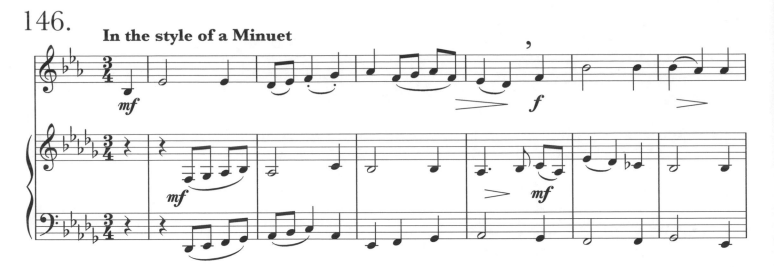

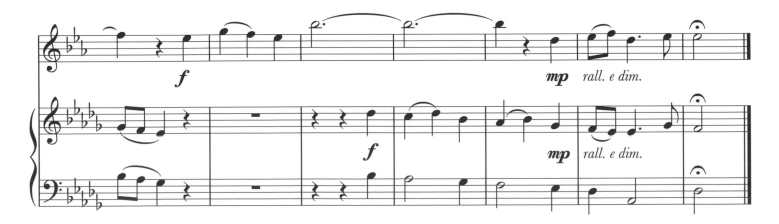

# Section 10 – Further transposition. Dance styles and whole notes

## Section 10 – Transposition (suite). Styles de danse et tons entiers
### Teil 10 – Weitere Transpositionen. Tanzstile und Ganztonleiter

Further examples for **transposition** are given which can also be read and played in the written keys as well. Previous sections can again provide additional material suitable for transposition.

**The main emphasis** is on exploring various dance forms, both old and new, and also in using **whole tone** tonality.

Other new features are the use of the **double sharp** (✗) and the introduction of **seven-time**. Think of these time signatures as 4+3 beats.

D'autres exemples de **transposition** sont donnés ici. Ils peuvent également être lus et joués dans les tonalités données. Les parties précédentes fournissent également des matériaux supplémentaires utilisables pour la transposition.

**L'accent principal** est mis sur l'exploration de différentes formes de danses, à la fois anciennes et récentes ainsi que l'utilisation de la gamme par tons.

Le **double dièse** (✗) et l'introduction de la mesure à **sept temps** sont d'autres nouveautés de cette partie. Pensez ces mesures selon le schéma 4+3.

Hier findest du weitere Beispiele zum **Transponieren**, die aber jeweils auch in der notierten Tonart gelesen und gespielt werden können. Weitere Stücke zum Transponieren findest du in den vorherigen Abschnitten.

**Der Hauptschwerpunkt** liegt auf der Betrachtung verschiedener alter und neuer Tanzformen sowie auf der Verwendung der **Ganztonleiter**.

Weitere neue Aspekte sind die Verwendung von **Doppelkreuzen** (✗) und die Einführung des **7/4- und 7/8-Takts**. Diese Taktarten können in 4+3 Schläge unterteilt werden.

*Performance directions used in this section.*

*Indications de jeu utilisées dans cette section :*

*Vortragsangaben, die in Teil 10 verwendet werden:*

| | | | |
|---|---|---|---|
| Adagio | slowly | lent | langsam |
| Allegro vivace | fast and lively | rapide et animé | schnell und lebhaft |
| Andante tranquillo | at a walking pace and peacefully | calme et modéré | ruhig schreitend |
| Calypso | a song from the Caribbean | chant des Caraïbes | karibischer Musikstil |
| Gavotte | a lively dance in compound time | danse animée en ternaire | lebhafter Tanz in zusammengesetzten Taktarten |
| Giocoso | playfully | joyeux | spielerisch |
| Grazioso | gracefully | gracieux | anmutig |
| Largo sostenuto | slow and sustained | lent et soutenu | langsam und gehalten |
| Tempo comodo | at a convenient tempo | à un movement à l'aise | in einem angenehmen |

# Section 10 – Further transposition. Dance styles and whole notes

Section 10 – Transposition (suite). Styles de danse et tons entiers

*Teil 10 – Weitere Transpositionen. Tanzstile und Ganztonleiter*

Transpose: Trumpet in A, C, D and E♭

Tranposez : trompette en *la*, *ut, ré* et *mi* bémol

Transponieren: A-, C-, D-, und Es-Trompete

**147.**

Transpose: Trumpet in A, C and D

Tranposez : trompette en *la*, *ut* et *ré*

Transponieren: A-, C-, und D-Trompete

**148.**

Transpose: Trumpet in A, C and D

Tranposez : trompette en *la*, *ut* et *ré*

Transponieren: A-, C-, und D-Trompete

**149.**

Transpose: Trumpet in A, C, D, E♭ and F

Transposez : trompette en *la*, *ut*, *ré*, *mi* bémol et *fa*

Transponieren: A-, C-, D-, Es-, und F-Trompete

## 150.

Transpose: Trumpet in A, C, D, E♭, E and F

Transposez : trompette en *la*, *ut*, *ré*, *mi* bémol, *mi* et *fa*

Transponieren: A-, C-, D-, Es-, E-, und F-Trompete

## 151.

Transpose: Trumpet in A, C, D, E♭, E and F

Transposez : trompette en *la*, *ut*, *ré*, *mi* bémol, *mi* et *fa*

Transponieren: A-, C-, D-, Es-, E-, und F-Trompete

## 152.

For additional pieces to transpose examples 153-161, as well as pieces in Sections 5 and 6 may be used

Les pièces des sections 5 et 6 ainsi que les exemples 153 à 161 peuvent être utilisés en guise de support à des exercices supplémentaires de transposition

Als weitere Stücke zum Transponieren können die Beispiele 153-161 sowie Stücke in Teil 5 und 6 verwendet werden

## 153.

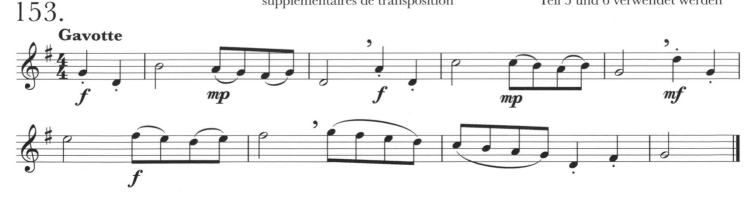

**154.**

**Gavotte**

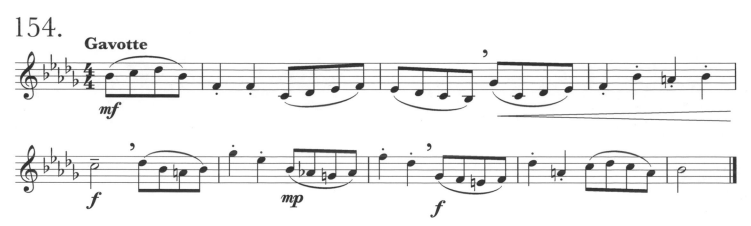

Whole tone (on E)            Gamme par tons entiers (*mi*)            Die Ganztonleiter (E)

**155.**

**Andante tranquillo**

**156.**

**Allegro vivace**

**157.**

**Gigue**

**158.**

**Calypso**

**159.**

**Cantabile**

68

Introducing 7-time · · · · · · · · · · · Introduction de la mesure à 7 temps · · · · · · · · · · · Einführung des 7-Takt

**160.**

*Gracioso*

**161.**

*Giocoso*

**162.**

*Adagio*

**163.**

**164.**

Tempo comodo

**165.**

Largo sostenuto

# Section 11 – All keys – double sharps and flats. Baroque to Atonal styles

## Section 11 – Toutes les tonalités – doubles dièses et bémols. Style baroque et atonalité

### *Teil 11 – Alle Tonarten – Doppelkreuz und - Be. Barock bis atonale Musik*

In this final section styles will range from **Baroque** to **Atonal**, and explore a variety of keys together with **double sharps** (×) and **double flats** (♭♭).

The range of notes extends from **low G** to **high C**.

*Performance directions used in this section.*

Dans cette section finale, les styles vont du **baroque** à la **musique atonale**, utilisant une variété de tonalités ainsi que le **double-dièse** (×) et le **double-bémol** (♭♭).

L'étendue des notes va du *sol* grave au *do* aigu.

*Indications de jeu utilisées dans cette section :*

Der letzte Teil enthält Stilrichtungen vom **Barock** bis zur **atonalen Musik** sowie verschiedene Tonarten mit **Doppelkreuzen** (×) und **Doppel-Bes** (♭♭).

Der Tonumfang erstreckt sich vom **tiefen G** bis zum **hohen C**.

*Vortragsangaben, die in Teil 11 verwendet werden:*

| | | | |
|---|---|---|---|
| Ad lib. | in free time | tempo au choix de l'interprète | frei wählbares Tempo |
| Allegro | fast | rapide | schnell |
| Allegro vivace | fast and lively | rapide et animé | schnell und lebhaft |
| Allegretto | moderately fast, but not as fast as Allegro | assez rapide qu'allegro | gemäßigt schnell |
| Allemande | a courtly dance with running semiquavers | danse de cour comportant des mouvements de doubles-croches | höfischer Tanz mit sechzehntelläufen |
| Andante con espressione | at a walking pace with expression | modéré et expressif | schreitend und ausdrucksvoll |
| Atonal | having no key note or tonality | sans tonique ni tonalité déterminée | ohne Grundton bzw. tonales Zentrum |
| Blues | a generally slow jazz style using a 'blues' scale | style de jazz généralement lent utilisant une échelle « blues » | meist langsamer Jazz-Stil unter verwendung der „Buestonleiter" |
| Con moto | with movement | avec movement | mit Bewegung |
| Latin | a South American style | style sud-américain | südamerikanischer Musikstil |
| Minuet | a classical dance in 3-time | menuet – courte et majestueuse danse à trios temps | kurzes, majestätisches Stück im 3/4-Takt |
| Molto allegro | very fast | très rapide | sehr schnell |

# Section 11 – All keys – double sharps and flats.
# Baroque to Atonal styles

Section 11 – Toutes les tonalités – doubles dièses et bémols.
Style baroque et atonalité

*Teil 11 – Alle Tonarten – Doppelkreuz und - Be. Barock bis atonale Musik*

## 166.

**168.**

Minuet

**169.**

Molto allegro

**170.**

**171.**

**172.**

**173.**

12 tone                    Musique sérielle dodécaphonique                    Tonreihe

**174.**

Atonal

Musique atonale

Atonal

## 175.

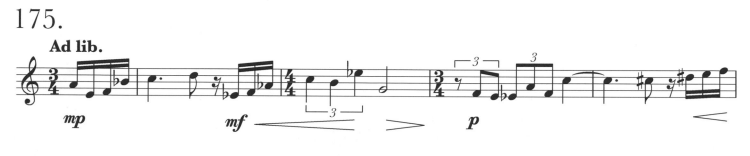

## 176.

**177.**

**178.**

**179.**

## 180.

**With a latin feel**

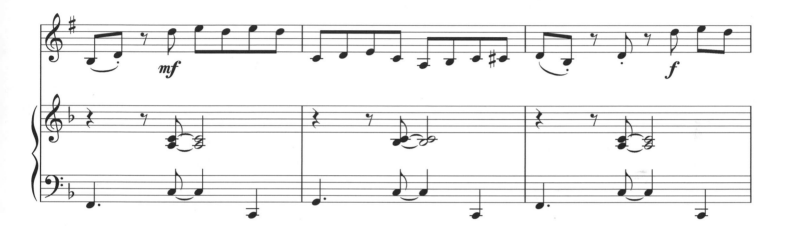

# Glossary
## Glossaire
### *Glossar*

Note performance directions together with their translations used throughout the book so that you have a complete list. Writing them down will help you to remember them.

Inscrivez ici les indications d'exécution utilisées dans ce volume et leur traduction pour en établir une liste complète. Le fait de les noter vous aidera à les retenir.

Schreibe hier alle Vortragsangaben, die im Buch verwendet werden, zusammen mit ihren Übersetzungen auf, so dass du eine vollständige Liste hast. Das Aufschreiben wird dir dabei helfen sie einzuprägen.

| Adagio | Slowly | Lent | Langsam |
|---|---|---|---|
|  |  |  |  |
|  |  |  |  |
|  |  |  |  |
|  |  |  |  |
|  |  |  |  |
|  |  |  |  |
|  |  |  |  |
|  |  |  |  |
|  |  |  |  |
|  |  |  |  |
|  |  |  |  |
|  |  |  |  |
|  |  |  |  |

| | | | |
|---|---|---|---|
| | | | |
| | | | |
| | | | |
| | | | |
| | | | |
| | | | |
| | | | |
| | | | |
| | | | |
| | | | |
| | | | |
| | | | |
| | | | |
| | | | |
| | | | |
| | | | |
| | | | |
| | | | |
| | | | |